Jezebel
Woman or the Spirit of Baal?

ISBN: 978-0-9904360-3-4 Softcover

This book was printed in the United States of
America.

Jezebel

Woman or the spirit of Baal?

Contents

Introduction   5

Chapter 1:   7   Understanding Jezebel
Chapter 2:   11   Jezebel the Idolater
Chapter 3:   13   Jezebel the Dominating Wife
Chapter 4:   15   Jezebel the Corrupt Tree
Chapter 5:   21   Jezebel a Treacherous Schemer
Chapter 6:   25   Jezebel Was Extremely Vain
Chapter 7:   29   The Death of Jezebel
Chapter 8:   35   Jezebel Number Two
Chapter 9:   39   The gods of Jezebel
Chapter 10:   43   Baal
Chapter 11:   47   Ashtoreth
Chapter 12:   53   Astarte: Canaanite Ishtar
Chapter 13:   55   Succoth-Benoth:
                    Babylonian Goddess
Chapter 14:   61   The Influence of Wicked Spirits

Introduction

The Jezebel spirit or the spirit of Baal?

These simple words evoke a sense of danger and a sort of mystical intrigue. Immediately the wicked wife of King Ahab comes to the forefront of our minds, producing a foreboding sense of extreme depravity. In essence, she has become the object of what a vile woman is.

Though Queen Jezebel was thoroughly reprehensible, it would be inconceivable to give her undue credit by considering her a strongman. There was an evil spirit at work in the life of Jezebel. This evil spirit is the strongman which continues to work through and against people today. In order to understand the spirit behind Jezebel we must understand who Jezebel was.

As we read **1 and 2 Kings** we clearly see the religious conflict between the worship of Jehovah and Baalim. For twenty-seven years Jezebel attempted to do away with the God of Israel and His prophets. She endeavored to replace the faith of Israel with the faith of her people, the Phoenicians.

Just like the Phoenicians she worshipped Molech.

Her faithfulness to her gods was greatly influenced by her father, Ethbaal King of Phoenicia. Ethbaal had a particularly strong religious zeal since he had been a high priest of Astarte before becoming king. When Jezebel married Ahab king of Israel, it formed an unholy political alliance between the small but influential seafaring kingdom and the Hebrew nation.

The resulting impact was the *murder of the innocent* to obtain whatever was desired and the moral decay of a nation whose god was the one true God. The spiritual strongman *behind* Jezebel gave her a manipulative strength over her already weak husband to do what he would not naturally have the confidence or courage to do.

1

Understanding Jezebel?

In **1 Kings 16:29** we begin the history of the thirty-two year reign of Ahab after his father Omri dies. Ahab did more evil in the sight of the Lord than any king before him.

1 Kings 16:31 is a good explanation of the root of this king of Israel's evil actions. He marries Jezebel the daughter of Ethbaal king of Phoenicia or Sidon.

Ethbaal's name meant **'with him is Baal'** or **'Baal's man'**. His name depicted the devotion towards his god, and he continued in his wholehearted loyalty to *Baal* in naming his daughter Jezebel.

There was no comparison with what her name meant and her true nature. Jezebel meant 'chaste, free from carnal connection.' Her character was completely the opposite of her given name. Instead of being chaste and free from carnal connection she used her beauty and charms to manipulate men into doing what she wanted.

The Phoenicians were great sailors and the best seafaring people of their time. Though they were great masters of the seas they were extremely idolatrous. To them the God of Israel was just another local god, a god of the land. The names of their gods were Baal and Ashtoreth or Astarte, and with these gods were a large number of false prophets.

When Ahab aligned himself with the Phoenicians in marriage to Jezebel, he adopted their gods as his and caused the people of Israel to follow after these gods as well. In fact he personally installed 450 false prophets to be priests and placed them in the magnificent temple of the sun god he had built in Samaria.

King Ahab and Queen Jezebel! He was weak-kneed, cowardly and fearful while she was manipulative, strong-willed, arrogant and full of self-importance. What made them unite? It couldn't have been spiritual beauty which caused King Ahab to lust after the voluptuous Jezebel. It was her physical beauty that ensnared him and the strength of her forceful character.

Jezebel, on the other hand, spotted a very weak and spineless king whom she could manipulate into doing her will. It was an opportunity to drive Jehovah out of Israel and set up Baal's worship thereby spreading the Phoenician religion farther.

The downfall of Ahab through his association with Jezebel has happened to many men in the Bible before him. Adam listened to Eve and sin came into the world. Samson lusted after Delilah and in spite of his great strength became a blind slave and eventually lost his life. Before being blinded by fire he was blinded by the beauty of Delilah. David the great king of Israel and a man after God's heart was blinded by a woman's beauty. Solomon the wisest man who ever lived was spiritually blinded because of his heathen wives. Joseph, however, was the only one smart enough to run from the seductive wife of Potiphar.

No other sin Ahab did could equal this great rebellion against the laws of God by taking Jezebel as his wife.

It is stated in historical records that for sixty years idolatry had tremendous advancement in the lives of the Hebrew nation.

The worship of idols meant more to the Israelites than the commandments of Jehovah. Idol worship produced the decaying corruption and moral disintegration of the Hebrew's way of life. Jezebel didn't just want to introduce idolatry to Israel she wanted to drive Jehovah completely out of Israel and destroy the worship of God.

Her name has now become synonymous of seductive power worldly deception and the worst form of wickedness.

Jezebel was no ordinary woman. She possessed an extraordinary power which manifested wherever she went and drew attention away from all others.

The attractive personality was NOT because of righteous morals; instead, she was empowered with such a strong force of character that her terrible destiny rivaled no other woman in scripture.

While the scriptures do not go into great description of her personality it simply sets forth the misdeeds and destruction that she was responsible for.

When we study her life we see the evidence of a dominating personality. The Bible shows no traces of a noble nature which makes a woman truly beautiful.

We must not under estimate her intelligence for she was exceptionally brilliant in a satanic sort of way. She cared nothing for higher restraint or higher principles. Cold-hearted and merciless this ice maiden plotted out her devilish schemes. Though a very talented woman, she perverted her talents to ensure the advancement of the kingdom of Baal. She was the protector and the watchman.

Using her gifts and strong personality she destroyed a king, her offspring, and she managed to pollute a Godly nation with the perversion of idol worship.

2

Jezebel the Idolater

Baal had a dedicated and faithful servant in Jezebel the Phoenician daughter to Ethabaal. None could match her zeal for Ashtoreth, the famous Zidonian goddess. She faithfully provided the everyday needs of hundreds of priests. Just how many priests she personally attended we're not quite sure; however, we do know of eight hundred fifty which were destroyed after the confrontation by the prophet Elijah on Mount Carmel.

It was easy to convert her husband's court to idolatry; although, it didn't bring her the satisfaction she longed for in her devotion to the god and goddess, Baal and Ashtoreth. She wanted the entire country to come under the influence of her gods. She had two heathen sanctuaries built, one in Samaria with four hundred fifty priests and the other in Jezreel with four hundred priests.

She embarked on a deadly mission to drive out the prophets of Jehovah from the land and secured her place in history as the first religious female persecutor. The fanatical religious enthusiasm inherited from her pagan father compelled her to exterminate all worship of the one and only true God. With such tenacity she almost succeeded.

This zealous advocate for Baal worship in Israel underestimated the God of the Hebrews. Jehovah rose up one of His true prophets, Elijah to confront King Ahab. He prophesied that for three years there would be no rain. Elijah was such a vocal champion for Jehovah Ahab referred to him as an enemy. Since Ahab was an enemy of God then Ahab was indeed Elijah's enemy.

When this prophet of God destroyed the eight hundred fifty prophets of Baal and Ashtoreth Ahab became afraid of Elijah and the power of Jehovah; however, Jezebel was not afraid. Instead she sent a message to the prophet Elijah that in one day's time he would be as dead as the false prophets he had just destroyed.

Terrified Elijah went into hiding. He knew Jezebel would do everything in her power to make sure her words would come to pass. Before you judge Elijah too harshly for his actions remember he was human and the evil power working within Jezebel made her far more formidable than King Ahab.

3

Jezebel the Dominating Wife

Ahab was putty in the hands of his domineering spouse. Jezebel was the lioness which roared out her commands, and Ahab was the wimpy mouse who obeyed. He could not stand against so strong a personality. Even the mighty Elijah feared her more than the king and his army. Because Ahab could not stand against her overbearing persona he was easily manipulated and controlled. It was no small feat for Jezebel to exert her will over her husband's and get her way.

Jezebel was so oppressive the scriptures show the army of Israel feared her more than Ahab. She was the dictatorial commander who never allowed her words to be broken. If any of her commands were not met someone would have to pay for this act of disobedience with their life. It was probable the unfortunate person's entire family would pay with their life as well. She cared for no one and used and abused everyone.

Though King Ahab may not have been as evil as his spouse he was just as guilty of all her crimes by not putting an end to what she was doing. He not only allowed her to enslave him, but he also allowed her to blaspheme the God of Israel and to enslave His people. Without the power and the authority of a king behind her Jezebel would still be a snake, but a snake without fangs. She was a deadly viper disguised as a woman who scoffed at any signs of righteousness or conscience in her husband, binding him with chains of evil which could not be broken.

Although she was a treacherous, evil, immoral, perverted and unrighteous human being without a conscience, we must not forget she was still only human. She was not a strongman of the spirit world; however, she was plainly controlled by one.

4

Jezebel the Corrupt Tree

In **Matthew 7:16-20** the Lord asks a question: "Do men gather grapes of thorns, or figs of thistles?" The Lord goes on to say a corrupt tree brings forth evil fruit and a corrupt tree cannot bring forth good fruit. What a ridiculous notion to think otherwise! I have never seen peaches growing on a pine tree, nor have I seen apples growing on a pecan tree.

Just like the corrupt tree, a person who does not know God cannot bring forth the fruit of the Spirit of God. Jezebel was rotten from the top of her head to the bottom of her feet. Because everything she touched became contaminated. She was power hungry and had no fear or respect for God's true holiness. Nothing was allowed to stand in the way of her desires. The fruit of this corrupt tree called Jezebel was dangerously poisonous.

2 Kings 9:22 proclaims Jezebel was not only a whore, but also a witch who was involved with spiritism. Ethbaal's corrupt nature passed to Jezebel and so did the rebellious nature of Jezebel pass to her own children. Each walked in arrogant rebellion against the only true God. The old adage: "The fruit doesn't fall far from the tree," would aptly describe the evil influence which affected generations after them.

Athaliah, whose name meant 'taken away by the Lord' or 'Jehovah has afflicted', manifested evil tendencies which Jezebel exhibited in her life. For Jezebel to have named her daughter Athaliah brought her own flesh and blood under a curse.

With the unfortunate circumstances of being King Ahab and Queen Jezebel's daughter, Athaliah naturally inherited her mother's depraved personality. In today's terms, she would be considered a sociopath. Continuing the legacy of her mother's Baal worship she extended the poison of idolatry into the veins of Jerusalem.

This mixture of Israelite and Phoenician married Jehoram the son of Jehoshaphat. Jehoram, unlike his father, was just as evil as his wife Athaliah. As soon as he secured his position as king he had all of his brothers who were loyal to Jehovah put to death by the sword. Though Jehoram did not slaughter to receive the throne like Omri Athaliah's grandfather, he certainly slaughtered to keep it intact. Like his father-in-law Ahab Jehoram found himself dominated by his evil scheming wife. However, Jehoram only reigned for eight years before dying of an incurable disease.

The union between Jehoram and Athaliah produced Ahaziah. With such a lineage this child proved to be more evil than his own mother Athaliah and his grandmother Jezebel. What chance did he have to be righteous with such influences! After his father died Ahaziah assumed the throne yet the power behind his throne was the same as it had been for his father's, Athaliah. She continued to destroy the worship of Jehovah and to establish Baal worship everywhere. Ahaziah was king for only one year and died from wounds received in battle.

When he died his mother Athaliah destroyed all of her grandsons except for one who was hidden from her in the house of God. Athaliah was now no longer the power *behind* the throne; instead, she asserted herself as the power *on* the throne and did so for six years. Her diabolical schemes to control the throne was motivated by the spirit operating behind her. It was the same spirit which controlled her mother Jezebel.

Who was the spirit? It was Satan, and he was working to destroy the leverage in which the Messiah, the seed of the woman would come. Athaliah like her mother was the slave of Satan and his plans. Although a daughter of a king, the wife of a king, and herself a queen, she died without being missed or mourned, just like Jezebel.

Jezebel also had a son named Ahaziah brother to Athaliah. His name meant 'Jehovah holds' or 'Jehovah possesses'. He reigned as the eighth king of Israel but for only two years. **2 Chronicles 20:37** states that Ahaziah was guilty of following the way of his father Ahab and his mother Jezebel. He worshipped the false gods of his mother. The scripture doesn't waste much time talking about this particular Ahaziah. **2 Kings 1:1-18** is the scant record of Ahaziah's dealings. He had fallen and became very ill so he sent men seeking answers from Baal-zebub to see if he would recover from his injuries.

As the men were going on their way to inquire of the god of Ekron, Baal-zebub, they were confronted by Elijah the prophet of Jehovah. Elijah told them to return to the king and tell him because he was seeking answers from Baal-zebub and not from Jehovah he would die. Therefore King Ahaziah sent a captain of his army with fifty men to bring Elijah the prophet to him. When the captain and his men got to the prophet God sent fire from heaven to destroy the captain and his men.

Instead of learning his lesson, the king sent another captain and his fifty men; nevertheless these men were also consumed by fire from heaven. Sin blinds men to the truth. Instead of repenting the king arrogantly sent another captain and his fifty men. This captain was unlike the other two before him. He did not become arrogant but humbled himself before the prophet. His life as well as the lives of his men was spared.

One hundred and two men died because of the arrogance of the king. Elijah went to the king and told him what Jehovah said. King Ahaziah died just as the man of God declared. Sadly Ahaziah was a product of his parents. His father Ahab, a victorious warrior, could have been known as a valiant man of God. Instead he was a cowardly hen-pecked husband, king, and idolater. His mother Jezebel was a daughter of a heathen king, a perverted idolater, and a despiser of righteousness.

Exodus 34:7 states God will punish the offspring of the unrighteous from three to four generations. Jezebel was a corrupt tree and her children and grandchildren were the evil fruit which continued to spread her poison and sinful rebellion. The Bible records Jezebel as a whore, a sorcerer, and a spiritualist. Though she possessed wealth and titles she died in absolute spiritual poverty. It's true she endeavored to bring down a nation meant to be a chosen vessel of honor for God; however, she was only human being, not a spiritual strongman.

5

Jezebel a Treacherous Schemer

The scheme to acquire the vineyard from Naboth was cold and calculating with no inkling of remorse.

Unfortunately for Naboth his vineyard happened to be right next to the palace of King Ahab and Queen Jezebel. He must have taken such great care of the vineyard for it to be so appealing to King Ahab. For someone who took great care with his land it is no wonder that Naboth's name meant prominence, illustrious, honored, respected and well known. What a stark difference in his personality with that of Ahab and Jezebel!

This man who had meticulously cared for the land which had been passed down to him was guilty of no wrongdoing except obeying God's law and having land next door to a spoiled covetous king. When Ahab saw Naboth's vineyard, he asked him for it. However, Naboth refused because it had been the inheritance of his fathers. The king understood why Naboth refused but he was childish and petulant; he simply went home to his bed and sulked.

Now, Jezebel was from a much different country than Israel and Judah. In her country under her father's leadership no one dared to refuse the request of the king. To say no to the king's wishes would result in their death as well as the destruction of their offspring. For her life had no value whatsoever. She did not care what she had to do to get her way, just like her father who killed his predecessor Phalles. Raised by a murderous conniving person like Ethbaal it is no surprise Jezebel reacted the way she did.

When she heard her husband was in bed having a pity party because Naboth refused to give him the vineyard she commanded him to get out of bed and to eat bread and make himself merry because she would obtain the vineyard for him. Immediately after she left Ahab she had letters written and sealed with the king's signet ring. These letters called for a public feast and demanded that Naboth be invited and placed above the people.

Once that was done, she hired the sons of Belial to bare false witness against him. They were to accuse him of blasphemy against God and the king. Then they were to take Naboth out and stone him until he died. What a terrible scheme! To kill anyone that stood in her way to get what she wanted was of little consequence to her.

Death of people did not trouble her in any way; therefore, when her husband died there was no mourning. Life meant nothing to her; only the fulfillments of her will was what mattered. Yet like most dictators she underestimated Jehovah God. She foolishly believed she was invincible, but God was about to show her otherwise.

He raised up Elijah to confront her husband, to let her know that God had judged him and would punish him for his cowardly deeds. The Lord also informed

King Ahab that He would deal terribly with Jezebel. She would not only die but dogs would drink her blood and eat her flesh. Then His judgment would pass to her son and daughter.

Jezebel was a wicked queen, a corrupt tree, an idolater and a treacherous schemer. In spite of her evil tyrannical rule she was still only a human and not a spiritual strongman. Who has the power to rise up and influence others to do his wicked and rebellious desires for generation after generation?

It's true Jezebel's children and grandchildren were wicked but they proved to be more so. There was definitely an evil spirit orchestrating the notes of Jezebel's life. It was the same wickedness behind Eve's decision to disobey God's command to eat the forbidden fruit.

It was also the evil behind Semiramis when she proclaimed herself as a goddess and took the title **'Queen of Heaven'**.

Just like Jezebel these women were not spiritual strongmen. They were the victims of the strongman.

This strongman is the one we are interested in uncovering, in order to protect our family, churches, homes and cities from this influence.

6

Jezebel Was Extremely Vain

As we see in **2 Kings 9:33-37**, the brutal deaths of Jezebel's husband, son and grandson were not enough to discourage her and bring her to repentance. Even though Elijah prophesied her death and what would happen to her when she died she was just as unable to fear her demise, as she was to feel remorse for any wicked deeds she had done. You would think while those who were close to her were dying she would closely examine her life and seek forgiveness. Sadly this was not the case. Being the extreme sociopath that she was nothing was more important than her desires. These aspirations dictated that she do what needed to be done, even if it involved death to achieve them.

She was definitely the spoiled princess daughter of a violent self-centered heathen king who worshipped Baal. There were very real evidences she possessed the attributes of both her earthly and her spiritual father. Her vanity knew no bounds even after she realized death was close at hand.

When she heard the sound of the horses carrying Jehu, the man chosen and anointed to fulfill the prophecy given by Elijah to destroy her and her wickedness, she took the time to arrange her hair and to paint her face. Perhaps as it has been said she knew she was going to die; therefore, she chose to die looking like a queen. However, I believe she was arrogantly confident of the control she had over the people. She literally believed no one would dare oppose her. Maybe she thought she was so glamorous that if she fixed her hair and painted her face she could seduce even Jehu, God's anointed vessel. Whatever the reason behind her quick toiletry she refused to be seen as a common woman.

After all she was a seducer a glamorous queen whom no man living could resist. To the eyes of Jehu and his army and even to the eunuchs who threw her out of the window to her death she was revolting. She appeared to them as she appeared to God a painted prostitute overshadowed by a spirit of witchcraft and spiritism.

Though her pride, ego, and wicked deeds were without equal only Satan was superior to her. No matter how many warnings came her way she refused to submit to the Lord God of Israel. If she didn't heed the Lord God of Israel then there was no surprise she would listen to man. As far as Jezebel was concerned no man was her equal, especially her superior.

It is definitely possible she was controlled by demons perhaps even demon possessed. Therefore, she could not spend thousands of years ensnaring women to be like her. Can you imagine what she could have done if she would have humbled herself and embraced the Lord God?

Jezebel was so blinded by her own sense of self-worth she could not see the greased pole she was on which led straight to hell. It's tragic how her vanity kept her from Jehovah's glorious kingdom and from a relationship with Him. All she managed to do was become the accepted synonym for wickedness. What a poor testimony to her pitiful life!

When you encounter those influenced by the spirit behind Jezebel, you do not have to fear.

Jehovah God within you is greater.

Neither should you hate the human vessel being controlled by this spirit. Rather pray for the person and perhaps God will use you to set her free.

7

The Death of Jezebel

The final confrontation came when God's chosen vessel Jehu arrived in the city. When he finally reached the palace he glanced upward and saw Jezebel with her hair up and face painted. He listened intently as Jezebel mocked him and called him a son of Zimri, indicating he was a drunken fool and not worthy of her attention. I am sure that Jezebel in arrogance and pride believed she was safe. No harm would come her way because the people were too afraid of her to even think of betraying her.

Jezebel's mocking insults to Jehu caused his anger to rise up inside of him. He saw two eunuchs standing behind the arrogant woman. He called out, "Who is with me? Who? Throw her down!" To Jezebel's horror and fear the eunuchs seized her and threw her out the window to the ground below.

When Jezebel hit the ground her blood splattered on the wall below her window. Though her death was murderous it was a fulfillment of God's prophecy to Ahab in **1 Kings 21:23, 24**. It was in Naboth's vineyard where Elijah delivered the message from God regarding the deaths of both Ahab and Jezebel.

Falling she could clearly see the soldiers with their spears, the horses which would trample her, and the dogs which were sent to eat her flesh. I wonder what went through her mind as she saw this. Did pride still bind her? Did she now understand that her rebellious arrogant nature separated her from the only One who could have helped her?

Her life is a stark testimony of **Romans 6:23** where the wages of sin is truly death physically and spiritually. Before her death her heart became hardened because of pride and her spiritual eyes became blind because of the rebellious spirit within an egocentric person.

Jehu and his army so despised Jezebel that he and his soldiers just trampled her body beneath the hooves of their horses. After riding over her they went into the palace to eat and drink.

When he finished his meal he remembered Jezebel and sent people out to bury her. After all she was a queen. Going to the place where she had fallen the men found only her skull, feet, and hands. While Jehu and his men ate the sumptuous palace food the dogs ate Jezebel. Tragic? Yes, however prophecy was fulfilled.

A valuable lesson learned here is: if God promised to bless you then you will be blessed. However, if God promises to curse you He will fulfill that promise. Jezebel's sins finally caught up to her and wages had to be paid. Thus the life of a tyrant, idolater, sorcerer and prostitute ended. Many people suffered under her reign of terror for so many years. I am sure the righteous probably wondered where God was during her time of dictatorial rule.

God always sees and knows what is happening to His people.

This statement is true, yet poses some questions:

- Where was His judgment as they suffered?
- Why didn't He come quickly to the aide of His people?
- Why didn't He remove this woman from power in Israel?

God's ways aren't our ways. He knows the perfect time to act and will not deviate from His divine plan. Just as in the case of rebellious Israel God waited for four hundred plus years to set them free. Despite their rescue from Egypt Israel continued in their rebellion against God and His prophets.

There was a time God allowed Israel to go through seventy years of enslavement to Babylon before He once again freed them. Were they grateful? Did they pledge their undying devotion to Jehovah?

No, they continued in their rebellion. Ironically there is a comforting train of thought in this. God is not willing for any man to perish but for all to come to the knowledge of Jesus as Lord. He will do what He has to do to bring a person or a nation to salvation and obedience.

What if the person or a nation continues to disregard God's warnings?

People have a will and it is not God's fault that judgment comes to them if they refuse to listen and obey. God is extremely patient and longsuffering when dealing with man or even a nation. He gives them a sufficient amount of time to turn from their evil ways.

Look at Jezebel! God gave her *twenty-seven years* to be committed to her husband as a faithful, loving, and supporting wife. He gave her twenty-seven years to put away Baal worship and to honor Him as the only true God and teach her children to follow His ways. It wasn't God's fault she refused His love and mercy.

Instead her decisions resulted in a death which seemed unimaginable. It was a divine retribution for her rebellion. She is recorded in history as one of the most deplorable, brutal, and evil women who ever lived. There is nothing about this wicked woman which could be considered good.

Jezebel stirred up Ahab but it was in the wrong direction. When a man marries a woman she can be a force for good and stand beside him, encouraging him to be a Godly man with strong morals. She can also be a force for destruction, leading him to ruin and ultimately destroying his life.

It is the same with parenting. A good woman will give her children exceptional guidance by imparting to them a Godly virtue.

She will teach them to love God and His word, to love people, and to respect authority. Jezebel did none of this. Her example was to terrify the people she ruled and to lead her husband and her children into idolatry. Her parental training led her children towards damnation.

Jezebel had all the traits of a demon spirit. She had the traits of one but it doesn't mean she was one. She was a human who was viciously evil and used as a pawn by Satan to pollute the Hebrews with idolatry. She died and was *never* resurrected as a spiritual strongman, leading women through the ages in rebellion and sin.

8

Jezebel Number Two

Revelation 2:18-29 is one reason people today believe that Jezebel the wife of Ahab is still active and spreading her rebellion to unruly women today. Even many strong Christians believe the Jezebel in **Revelation** is the daughter of Ethbaal. Their belief is that she is the spirit behind these domineering ladies. If that is the case then Ahab is the spirit behind the husband or pastor who submits to the controlling feminine personality of Jezebel within these women.

Why would they say these domineered men have the spirit of Ahab? Why not the spirit of Timothy? He had a problem standing up to domineering women. Paul had to rebuke and correct Timothy because of this weakness. We know Timothy is standing now in the presence of the Lord he served. Ahab is no more behind these men than Timothy is.

The truth is the spirit which had control of Ahab tried to control Timothy. It is that spirit which is alive and just as active as he was centuries ago.

Revelation 2:18-29 speaks about a woman named Jezebel. Let me make something perfectly clear: This is *not* the Jezebel of the Old Testament. Even though this Jezebel has all the attributes of the first Jezebel, she is a different person altogether.

In fact Walter Scott in his exposition of the book of Revelation explains that he felt this Jezebel in Revelation might not have been a person. Instead Jezebel in Revelation may be the rise of the papacy and the Roman Catholic Church, including its false documents and doctrines. As we look further into what Scott writes, we find a parallel between the two distinct Jezebels. The Jezebel of the Old Testament was a woman, a queen, an idolater, a persecutor, and the virtual ruler and director of the government of Israel. Her husband Ahab was putty in her hands.

Jezebel of the apocalypse is all this and more. Combining in her these and other features of the papal system **Revelation 17:18** she arrogantly assumes the title of a prophetess. She professes to teach with authority. Along with her teaching she applies all the arts and seduction of minds especially trained to affect her full purpose. Here 'mother church' is the cry of every member of the Roman Catholic Church. Walter Scott contends that the Roman Church is the Jezebel of the modern age.

It is quite evident in **Revelation 2** there was a group of people who were guilty of mixing the Christian truth with idolatrous necromancy in the church of Thyatira. This section of the church becomes antagonistic to the spiritual integrity of the real and truthful Christian faith. *Mr. Herbert Locker* also states that the conditions in Thyatira produced a sentimental fanaticism of indulgence where terrible wantonness and positive fornication grew. The name of Jezebel was given to this unworthy element in the church because of its resemblance between its perversion of truth and the idolatrous wife of King Ahab.

The word prophetess can mean a group of false prophets. The Hebrew feminine expresses collectively a multitude whose relationship to the church of Thyatira was like that of a wife to her husband. Both Scott and Locker present good points of view. However, I believe that the Jezebel of **Revelation** is actually devious, domineering, and controlling women with great influence in the church.

Who is the driving force behind the group who pride themselves in having an advanced theology of liberalism? All others are not as enlightened as they are; therefore, all others are inferior. This Jezebel and the groups which are submitted to her have a strong influence over the weaker Christian through the power of sorcery, prognostication, and lack of righteous morals. Mr. Locker does make a thought-provoking statement in his dispensation of his history of Jezebel. He states, "is it not interesting to see the influence this kind of woman has in starting false religions".

Look at the influence of women like Mary Baker Eddy, the founder of Christian Science, the Fov sisters, and Eleanor White, whose cult is still active in misleading people today. Because of the effects of this second Jezebel she has earned the title of the first prostitute, idolatrous sorcerer and queen of heaven.

The name Jezebel, as is the name Satan, will always be synonymous with wickedness and evil.

The influences of Jezebel one and Jezebel two on the people of God through generations are clearly seen. Ellicot phrased it best. It is most appropriate to view the name, Jezebel, as symbolical. This spirit behind the Jezebel of the Old Testament and the Jezebel of the apocalypse is proud. It has a self-constituted authority and vaunts claims of superior holiness or higher knowledge linked with a disregard of and perhaps a proud contempt for legalism, followed by open immorality. This spirit has been discovered again and again in the churches of God.

9

The Gods of Jezebel

Ethbaal the father of Jezebel was utterly devoted to Baal which proved the influence of his parents giving him the name meaning 'Baal man'. Not only did he serve Baal, but he also was a high priest of Astarte or Ashtaroth. He passed the legacy on to his daughter by naming her Jezebel after the false god Bel or Baal. With so much familial guidance is it any wonder Jezebel grew to be an idolater and sorcerer?

To become known as one of the most evil and wicked women in history she had to have had help from an evil supernatural entity. We have been emphasizing the point that there was a controlling spirit behind Jezebel and this spirit still wrecks havoc today. In actuality it comes from our adversary Satan. However, he is revealed through a conglomeration of false gods.

There is, a Babylonian god and a version of Enlil. Enlil according to legend was also called Ellil, meaning god of the earth.

He was a Mesopotamian god who was so powerful that no other gods could look at him. Supposedly he was a child of An, heaven and Ki, earth. Being a child of both he chose earth for his domain.

He was considered the patron deity of Nippur in Mesopotamia. Enlil dethroned Anu who was a horn-headed god. This horn-headed god was symbolic of ruler ship and royalty. Anu was also know by the Sumerians as An. He was the overlord of the gods and their protector.

Enlil overthrew Anu, and in turn Enlil was overthrown by Bel. The daily worship offering to Bel was forty sheep, twelve great measures of fine flour, and six vessels of wine. This false god had quite an appetite. In addition to Bel the people of Sidon/Phoenicia also worshipped Eshmun, the god of health and healing and called him Adonai. He was identified with the Greek Asclepius, and the Greeks called him Adonis.

It is an interesting fact that Bel the great god of Babylon and Phoenicia had his roots in man. Ninus, which was one of the many names given to Nimrod, was believed to be the son of Bel. Nimrod was not a Nephilim. His father was human and not a fallen angel. Why then was Nimrod called the son of Bel?

Let's begin with Cush, the grandson of Noah and the father of Nimrod. Cush was the ringleader in the great apostasy after the flood. He was known as Bel or Belus for a short time and then was replaced by his son, Nimrod. Cush was also known by the Egyptian synonym as Her-mus or Mercury which simply means 'the son of Ham'. He was the original prophet of idolatry.

The controlling spirit behind Jezebel was the same spirit operating behind Cush, his son Nimrod and his wife Semiramis.

Though both Cush and Nimrod were proclaimed to be gods we know they were only men being manipulated by a spiritual strongman. By exploring other gods Jezebel worshipped we find a pattern that reveals the spirit *behind* the wicked woman.

10

Baal

The name Baal, the god of Babylon and Phoenicia simply means 'lord' or 'master'. It was more of a title rather than a name. You must understand that the true names of many of the gods as well as the strongmen of the spiritual kingdom were kept secret. In many cultures the true birth name of a person is never revealed to anyone outside of the immediate family. If you know the true name of your adversaries you would have power over them.

The purpose behind having the names of a god being kept secret was having an unfair advantage. It was believed if someone found out the name of a deity the fortunate person could gain favor with this god and take his attention away from his normal worshippers. Knowing the secret name of the gods could be dangerous in the hands of the enemy.

The local gods of Babylon were called Baal. The greatest of Baal dates from the Phoenician settlement of the Eastern coast of the Mediterranean empire where they migrated from Negev. This Baal was an enemy of El the greatest god of the time. He was called Baal Tsaphon, lord of the north and also Baal Lebanon. It was thought that his real name was Adad or Hadad, the weather god or god of thunder. According to mythological history this would make his mother Asherat the goddess of the sea.

He is shown wearing the great horn helmet and spearing the earth. Remember the larger the horns the more power belongs to the one wearing them.

He is also shown in allegorical carvings grasping a tree which he is about to strike with a club. Both of these images are symbolic of lightning. This Baal, known as the great Baal, was the father of Mot, the harvest god and Aleyin, the Phoenician god of springs and vegetation. These twin brothers were always fighting with one another. Baal was also the father of Anat, an earth goddess and sister of Aleyin and Mot. Not only was she an earth goddess, but she was also a warrior goddess who was responsible for the murderous slaying of her brother Mot.

Legend states that Anat also known as Qadesh, meaning 'holy' was linked to the lion. In a highly evocative description of her dealings with Mot she first set her dogs on his flock, killed him with a sickle, beat him with a flail, roasted him in a fire, ground him up and finally scattered the debris over the fields. Then El created monsters which attacked and killed Baal. This highly volatile god family of Baal was the one Jezebel worshipped.

Studying Baal we discover there were other gods known as Baal. The Baal most commonly seen in scriptures was Baal Shamin or Beelsamin, lord of the skies.

The Baal worshipped in Tyre was originally a solar god who acquired nautical attributes as a god of an important trading port. He was otherwise known as Melkart or Melech, king of the city.

This last title simply means **Moloch**, god to whom *children were sacrificed* and whose priests Elijah slew with righteous fury. The Baal worshipped in Sidon was Eshmun, god of health. In Carthage, a colony of the Phoenicians, they worshipped Baal Hamon or Baal Ammon. The Romans adopted this Libyan god later as Jupiter Ammon. He was a sky and fertility deity whose animal was the ram.

Is it any wonder we find Jezebel's nature so rebellious and idolatrous? The gods she worshipped exhibited and encouraged this kind of behavior.

Closer study of these gods and goddesses shows again and again the perverted acts of incest between father and daughter, as with Baal and Anat, and with Diana and her brother as well as with her son. This perversion was manifested in the life of Ethbaal and his daughter Jezebel.

11

Ashtaroth

Ashtoreth is recognized by other names such as Ishtar, Ashtort, Ashtoreth, Astarte, Anatis, Anat, Atar and Isis. She is considered the Mesopotamian goddess of love and fertility and her father was Sin or Shamash, the Mesopotamian moon god. In Ur he was known as Nanor or Nanna and was one of the first rank of gods. Sin formed the main triad with Shamash, the sun and Ishtar, goddess of love.

He was described as an old man with a long beard and every night he sailed the sky in his boat. When the moon was full it was described as his crown. When the moon was crescent-shaped it was thought as his weapon or his boat. Sin was the enemy of evil spirit. In fact he was the enemy of all those who would use night to cloak their evil deeds. Once, according to legend, he was eclipsed by a rebellion formulated by evil spirit and was saved by Marduk.

Sin was wise, secretive, and full of good counsel and he was considered the measure of time. He was also believed to be the son of Enlil and Ninlil. His own children were Shamash, the sun god and Ishtar, goddess of love and fertility. Shamash the son of Sin was not only the brother of Ishtar, but he was also her husband. Incest was quite popular among the gods and goddesses. For example: Diana had relations with her brother Dionysus and later with her own son.

In Egypt the god and goddess, Osiris and Isis were brother and sister as well as husband and wife.

Shamash, the sun god was honored and worshipped in Mesopotamia, in Sippar, and in Larsa. Also revered as the god of divination, he was known for his wisdom. His symbol was a saw which he used to cut decisions with. Omniscient and all seeing his rays were thrown over all the earth as a net.

He lived in the mountain of the earth. Every morning the great door of his palace was thrown open by scorpion men. Armed with his saw, Shamash mounted his chariot which was kept waiting for him by his chauffeur Bunene. Together they would set off for their day journey across the sky. At night Shamash entered another great door located in the mountains of the west and traveled unseen through the earth until he was once again in the mountains of the east.

Shamash is displayed as a four-rayed sun or as a winged disc representing the sun. His sons were Kittum, god of truth and Misharum (Mishayim), god of justice. The Arabic word for sun is **Sams** and the Sumerian name for Shamash was **Utu.** Some even try to attach the story of Samson to Shamash. The secret of Samson's strength and the cutting of his hair sounds like a sun story.

Ashtoreth to the Phoenicians was the goddess of love and fertility. As is so often the case she controlled the negative as well as the positive side of her particular domain. Therefore, she was not only the radiant sweet and delightful goddess of love; she was also the stern and cruel goddess of war. Thus she bore the title 'lady of sorrows and battles' as well as the 'lady of heaven'.

To the spiritually adolescent human mind Ashtoreth rang absolutely true as the adored cruel object of youthful desires. The main shrine of her worship was located in ancient Uruk or Erech where sexual acts were performed as an offering to the gods. The part of the goddess was performed by the high priestesses and the part of her consort was played by the high priest king who was their carnal partner symbolically slain in imitation of the death and resurrection of the god.

Ashtoreth in her identity of Ishtar was very dangerous to men. Her passion would cause men to become vulnerable. Even animals were weakened and could easily be trapped and domesticated.

The hero Gilgamesh was the center of her attention for a while. He refused her advances for a while which took great courage to do so. Usually all her lovers would end up being transformed into animals. Gilgamesh insured his own death by refusing Ishtar's sexual advances.

Ishtar or Ashtoreth is considered the original femme fatale. Once she locked her eyes on you there was no chance of escaping.

She was worshipped in Babylon where a magnificent gate is named for her. She was identified with Ninlil who was the consort of Enlil. Ninlil was considered a mother goddess, an earth goddess, and a fertility goddess as well. Most pictures of Ishtar or Ashtoreth show her wearing a necklace of lapis lazuli which was very sacred to her. She also carried a bow and arrow while standing on the back of a lion.

It was said that she caused the death of Tammuz, the sun god.

Tammuz was the son of Nimrod and Semiramis. Ashtoreth was so lethal that anyone sampling her lover would ultimately die. She is also identified with the planet Venus. In fact her vibrant character can be traced to all the religious cultures of the world in some form or fashion.

This goddess with a licentious nature who would get her way by sexual favor or murder was extremely dominant. All men either submitted to her wiles or died. Now we can plainly see who the power behind Jezebel was.

The attributes of her gods and goddesses were manifesting as the fruits of her flesh.

These goddesses are really just one entity

Inanna	Ishtar
Sumerian	Assyro-Babylonian (Semitic)
Queen of the gods, Earth Mother Love, fertility, and battle goddess	Earth, moon, love, fertility, and battle goddess
Seasonally dying for lover, Dumuzi	Seasonally dying for lover, Tammuz

Astarte/Ashtoreth
Phoenician
Love and fertility goddess
Seasonally dying for lover, Adoni

Atergatis/Athirat	Aphrodite/Venus
Philistine/Syrian Canannite	Cypriot/Greek Roman
Fertility and wisdom goddess	Love goddess
Seasonally dying for Baal	Seasonally dying for lover, Adonis

These different goddesses of different nations and cultures can all be traced back to one entity and it is not the human woman named Jezebel.

It is *Semiramis* the wife of Nimrod, the mighty hunter before God.

12

Astarte: Canaanite Ishtar

Astarte, also known by the Greek form Ashtart, is regarded as the chief goddess of fertility in Tyre and Sidon. Therefore she is simply the same entity as the goddess Ishtar. In fact Astarte also merges with Asherat, Anat, and with the Egyptian goddess, Hathor. She came to Egypt and Ramesses II had a temple built for her. It was said she and the Egyptian goddess Isis were best friends. Like Anat and Hathor, Astarte was a suckler of kings and like Ashtoreth was associated with the planet Venus.

The Greeks transferred her role to their version of the goddess, Aphrodite. In London, Carlisle, Corbridge, and Northumberland during Roman time there was a cult of Astarte and Tyrian Herakles which were served by priestesses. This cult probably existed as they were connected with the presence of Eastern traders.

The symbols of Astarte are the sun, moon, stars, the lion, the bull, the snake, the dove and the horse.

She was considered the power behind the sun and moon. Actually this queen of the gods and goddesses was the sex and warrior goddess, the mother of all living. In essence Astarte was the same as Ashtoreth and Ishtar. This goddess, as well as Baal and Bel, are simply different manifestations of the same evil spirit.

It was the evil spirit behind Semiramis, the wife of Nimrod and it was the evil spirit behind Jezebel, the wife of Ahab. It will also be the evil spirit behind the future Jezebel known as the whore of Babylon, the mother of all harlots. This evil spirit will be behind the false religious system founded by the false prophet and the antichrist that is to come.

13
Succoth-Benoth: Babylonian Goddess

According to the <u>Unger Bible Dictionary</u>, page 417, Succoth-Benoth was an idol set up in Samaria (**2 Kings 17:30**) by displaced Babylonians. This divinity has been identified with Zarpanitum, the consort of Marduk, the major god of the Babylonians. He has also been connected to the Akkadian expression, *sakkut binuti*, the supreme arbiter of the world. This is a construed title of Marduk and the form Succoth-Benoth represents the Hebraization of it.

The title Succoth-Benoth really means the booths or tents of the daughter brothels. They were idolatrous tents for impure purposes. Temple prostitutes used these booths to sacrifice to their goddesses. *Alexander Hislop states in his book, <u>The Two Babylons</u>,* that the name Succoth-Benoth has frequently been supposed to be two words, and to refer to booths or tabernacles used in Babylon for infamous purposes like prostituting.

Clericus refers to the rabbins as being of the same meaning here; however, the contexts clearly show that the name Succoth-Benoth must be the name of an idol. How is it that the nations made gods of their own choosing? They put them in houses in the high places which the Samaritans had made in every city of the nations they abided in. Scriptures say the men of Babylon made Succoth-Benoth, which was an idol-symbolizing woman and motherhood.

Succoth refers to tabernacles or tents, while *benoth* signifies at once to bring forth children. The two names together meant the tent of childbirth or building up houses. These two names which were the names of two goddesses were the supposed fulfillment of the pagan prophecy of the two mothers who would give birth to the savior seed.

Bacchus was supposedly the fulfillment of the savior seed. Legend states while he was still an embryo in his mother, Semele he was rescued from the flames which killed his mother. After being saved he was sewn into the thigh of Jupiter, the father of the gods and goddesses. Though he was conceived by Semele he was brought forth by Ino. With his birth the triad was formed. This trinity was accepted in all religions and cultures of the world.

This triad was not the trinity of the Christian Bible but was a trinity consisting of two women and a son. There is a similarity with the gods in Egypt where Nepthys conceives Osiris under the name Anubis who is adopted and brought forth by Isis. Then Isis conceives Horus, the male sun god who is brought forth by Nepthys.In Babylon Hera is the conceiver, Rhea the one bringing forth, and the male child is Zeus.

What a perversion of the triune God! In relation to the trinity of the Bible, the Father, Son, and Holy

Spirit, we now have a deviant one consisting of the mother that conceives, the mother that brings forth, and the son.

At one time in Rome, it was Juno, Minerva, and Jupiter. Later it became Juno, Fortuna, and Jupiter-puer which was the boy child, Jupiter. Finally after the Tarquins were expulsed, Rome built a magnificent temple to the triad Ceres, Libera, and Liber – two mothers and a son. This sort of triad led people to worship different goddesses as the author of creation.

In the philosophy of many religions, the woman is the seed-bearer and the life-giver; therefore, it must be so. In the act of creation the goddesses conceive the seed and bring forth the child. These gods and goddesses of Sion, Phoenicia, and Babylon became a part of the human, Jezebel.

After all, she was raised worshipping these false gods. Just as a Christian is truly transformed into the new life and comes under the Lordship of Jesus Christ, he or she begins to reflect the fruits and attributes of God. The more a person surrenders to God the more of God is reflected in him. This same principle can be applied to Ethbaal and Jezebel.

Ethbaal, 'the man of Baal' or 'he who is like Baal' was so devoted to his god that wherever he went people could see the nature and attributes of Baal manifested through him. His daughter Jezebel, the wife of Ahab was just as zealous in her worship.

She was so devoted to Baal and Bel worship that she became an open vessel completely surrendered to him to be used as he so desired.

She personally fed 450 priests of Baal at her table daily. Her husband Ahab gave the order to build a magnificent temple to Jezebel's gods and appointed 400 priests to minister there. The only god not allowed in Israel at this time was the great Jehovah the God who delivered and kept safe the people of Israel.

The situation in Israel at that time was like the current conditions in America. The leaders of our country have opened the door to any false god which accompany people coming to this land. No god is refused entrance except the God who made this country great, the only true God, the God of the Bible, our Adonai Elohim. The Lord God who loved us so much He gave His only Son so we could be reunited with Him forever.

With Jezebel who was completely devoted to her gods. You could see the presence of these false gods working through her.

So it is today with our country's leaders!

You can see the presence of the power of darkness working through them.

Although there is only one antichrist who will be the last evil dictator of the world, there are still many leaders of the governments of the world who are already submitted to his spiritual influence throughout the world that opposes God and his word.

My advice to all believers and all who read this book

To keep your eyes on Assyria and on Turkey for the future world dictator will soon be making his appearance from that area.

Jezebel was truly wicked and evil yet we have to understand she was just a human being.

She may have influenced the generation she lived and ruled in as well as her son, daughter and grandchildren, but she was only mortally human

14

The Influence of Wicked Spirits

Jezebel was truly wicked and evil yet we have to understand she was just a human being. She may have influenced the generation she lived and ruled in as well as her son, daughter and grandchildren, but she was only mortally human.

You could rightly say she was a strong spiritual influence over the people while she was alive. However, the moment she used her ability to personally influence the coming generation her life came to an end. Her life ended but her evil reputation has been manifested in others throughout the generations.

Hitler inspired people to perform hate crimes in honor of his name and to spread the hate and suffering throughout the world. Today if someone is arrested for hate crimes we don't say the person is possessed with the spirit of Adolf Hitler.

We say he was greatly influenced by the actions and words of Hitler.

We know that spirit who compelled Hitler to act in the perverse insane ways he did was one of the devil's choice strongmen. This strongman drove Hitler deeper and deeper into the satanic darkness of hate and prejudice against God's people. Hitler was responsible for the death of six million Jews and many millions of Christians, as well as many brave service personnel who stood courageously against his juggernaut of evil and his desire to control the world.

We cannot say when a person acts out in devilish ways whether he or she is possessed by the spirit of Hitler. We can say he was influenced by the actions and words of Hitler and the spirit which drove Hitler to perform wicked acts is now working through the life of this person. When we try to cast out this spirit, we do not rebuke the spirit of Hitler; instead, we take authority over the spirit operating behind and with Hitler.

This is where it is vital you have the gift of discernment. The Lord by His Holy Spirit may reveal to you the specific name of this spirit and when you call it by its name he cannot hide any longer and must obey the name of Jesus. The Lord may not choose to give you the name of the spirit but may simply speak to your spirit and say, "This spirit is the same spirit who was behind Hitler, Alexander the Great, Pharaoh or Nimrod."

Yes, this spirit has for centuries been manifesting himself, his will, and his desire through world leaders both male and female. He has been responsible for enslaving an entire nation. He has established devil worship in many countries and turned many away from the God of creation. He has been behind the worst crimes of the centuries. He has used mass murders to do his will. He is the false god, Molech or

Marduk. This spirit has slaughtered millions of infants still in their mothers' wombs. Yes, these spirits are very real and the Bible warns us about them. They have a leader and his name is Satan, or as the Hebrews call him, the Adversary.

These unclean spiritual strongmen obey him completely. They are all assigned to different areas of the world. It is their goal to bring the entire earth under the rule of their satanic majesty. Like Satan or Lucifer all these strongmen have names. Many of their names are the names of the false gods of the nations in the Old Testament. For instance, gods like Chiun, Dagon, Marduk, Molech, Baal, Bel, Beelzebub and Belial, and goddesses like Ashtoreth, Astarte, Isis, Elstha, Venus, Aphrodite, Diana, Hecate and Hera are the names in which the strongmen chose to reveal themselves to man.

You have other names which are descriptive like leviathan, behemoth, Rahab, the spirit of Egypt, the dragon, and the whore of Babylon. Under the authority of these strongmen are an innumerable amount of demons who help to enslave mankind and bring about the kingdom of Satan on the earth.

Therefore, when you have a person or persons in your fellowships or churches who are acting just like Jezebel or the spirit of Ahab is manifested in them.

Do not be misled and believe it is really Jezebel and Ahab. It is the same spirits who worked behind and through Jezebel, Ahab, Nimrod, Semiramis,

Hitler, or any other dictator, mass murderer, child abuser, or rapist.

Never take to yourself a battle against one of these spiritual strongmen. Wait until you hear from God. For if you go in your own strength the battle is yours and you will lose. However, if the Lord sends you He will equip you and give you everything you need, including the name of your adversary and the victory.

In these days of darkness we can see the return of the ancient spirits who used to be worshipped as gods. We are certainly living in the times of Noah where every man did what was right in his own eyes and worshipped whatever gods he wanted. It was a time so wicked that it provoked God to anger and he vowed to destroy the whole world.

We are in the days of Sodom and Gomorrah where the stench of their wickedness covered the throne of God.

It was a time where witchcraft, homosexuality, and the neglect of the poor were rampant. The men of the towns of Sodom and Gomorrah were so perverted that no man was safe. These men were so much under the influence of these ancient gods that not even the angels were safe from their ungodly lust.

These days are back. Men are free to worship any god as long as it isn't the God of creation. We cannot even call sin 'sin' anymore.

If we stand up and side with the Holy Scriptures and then speak the truth we can be charged with hate crimes and jailed without a trial.

Who is the real enemy behind Jezebel?

The spirit of Jezebel has not returned, but the spirit behind her has and that is who your real enemy is. **Baal** and **Bel** have come to America and these ancient spirits have come back to claim a new kingdom.

We do not need the return of Elijah; instead, we need the return of the spirit which was with Elijah.

The ancient Spirits were behind the prophets of Baal and Bel

Without God's spirit we cannot defeat the ancient spirits which were behind the prophets of Baal and Bel.

We must have God's spirit, so America can once more be a nation under God, a righteous nation.

My prayer is: *O God, please return.*

Give us not what we deserve, which is judgment, but instead O Lord, grant us mercy for Your great Namesake.

Forgive us our sin and teach us the right way to live, so that once again we will be one nation under God, a nation of people committed to You and Your kingdom purpose.

Products

Books

A Quest for Spiritual Power - Redeemed from the
Curse - testimonial
Choisi Par Le Maitre: En quête de puissance
spirituelle - French translation
A Quest for Spiritual Power - Arabic translation
Nimrod - How religions began and how it applies
today
Spiritual Opposition to the Five Fold Ministry
The Secret Names of the Strongmen - study material
& prayer manual
Jezebel - human or the spirit of baal?
The Dispensation of the Lion and the lamb
The Return of the Days of Noah

Available on Amazon

About the Author

Dr. Henry Lewis is the President of an Apostolic International ministry called Joshua International. Joshua International offers Biblical Leadership Training and Spiritual Over comers material. Henry Lewis is a Sicilian Jew and a descendent of Andrew Murray.

He is married to his wife, Patricia, for over 42 years. They have been in ministry since 1980 and have two children.

Dr. Lewis has authored 10 books. The first book called A Quest for Spiritual Power is now translated in Arabic and in French. The Arabic book was printed in Egypt and the French book was put together in Switzerland and printed in France.

Dr. Lewis is a sought-after speaker and author, teaching at churches and conferences along with numerous TV guest media outlets teaching on subjects such as: spiritual warfare, revival, transformation, revelation, transformational prayer. Henry evangelizes and teaches with international prophetic leaders in 10 countries.

His testimony of his former occult leadership experiences of seven generations has enabled him to share the love of God and his delivering power.

Charisma magazine shared is testimony in 2000. 750,000 Hindus translated the article in their language and accepted Christ.

Dr. Lewis attended several colleges which led to obtain three Doctorates in Counseling, Theology and Christian Education.

Henry and his wife have established churches in the US. Their first church was by the assistance of Aimee Semple McPherson's son, Rolf McPherson, who believed in their calling. Later, Dr. Roy Hicks, Sr. (friend who worked at Angelius Temple with Rolf McPhearson) supported them as well.

Henry and Patricia's spiritual foundation was formed from: Dr. Leonard Heroo (Apostle and President of Zion Bible Institute), McPherson), Evangelist Robert Schambach, Prophet David Wilkerson and Derek Prince, Lester Sumrall etc.

Henry's passionate thirst for the knowledge and truth of God's word led him to obtain a deep relational experience with his Lord and Savior, Jesus Christ – and not a religion – so he could hear and know the voice of God.

His vision is to teach and train a courageous generation the incorruptible Word of God and introduce the power of the Holy Spirit. Henry and Patricia's goal is to bring restoration to all nations including the Native Americans. His wife, Patricia is of the Iroquois nation.

Henry & Patricia coordinated large transformation events in New England under the 'Vision for New England" network which began in Salem, Ma with the help of Rev Ken Steigler & local pastors. Daystar programming promoted the events for 2 years. A transformation video was edited that shares the signs and wonders and miracles that occurred.

Dr. Henry Lewis is ordained with the Assemblies of God. Henry is also ordained Rabbi through Asher Intrater from the Revive Israel Ministries

He is available for speaking.

Jezebel

For More Information

In the US write:

H.A.Lewis
Joshua International

P.O. Box 1799
Maricopa, AZ 85139

Email: Info@halewis.org
Email: Info@ joshua-edu.org

To order or inquire of additional products, visit us online

Website: www.halewis.org
Visit us on face book

Book Cover Artist: Debbie Wheat
Contact: izayu54@yahoo.com

Book Co-coordinators

Grace Miller
Patricia Lewis

Jezebel